FOREWORD BY
Allen Ginsberg

INTRODUCTION BY
Thich Nhat Hanh

TRANSLATED BY
YOUNG-MOO KIM AND
BROTHER ANTHONY OF TAIZÉ

What?

108
Zen
Poems

KO UN

PARALLAX PRESS
Berkeley, California

PARALLAX PRESS
P.O. Box 7355
Berkeley, California 94707
www.parallax.org

Parallax Press is the publishing division
of Unified Buddhist Church, Inc.

Korean names and words are printed according to the Revised Korean Romaniza-
tion (RKR) system. Chinese names and words are printed according to the pinyin
romanization system.

Cover and text design by Jess Morphew.
Cover calligraphy and interior art by the author.
Translated from the Korean by Young-Moo Kim and Brother Anthony of Taizé.
Parallax Press would like to thank Clare You for her language expertise.

Library of Congress Cataloging-in-Publication Data
Ko, Un, 1933-
  What? : 108 Zen poems / Ko Un ; translated by Kim Young-Moo and Brother
Anthony. -- [Rev. ed.].
    p. cm.
  Rev. ed. of: Beyond self. 1997.
  ISBN 978-1-888375-65-7
  1. Ko, Un, 1933---Translations into English. 2. Zen poetry, Korean--Translations
into English. I. Ko, Un, 1933- Beyond self. II. Title. III. Title: 108 Zen poems.
  PL992.42.U5A2 2006
  895.7'14--dc22

                              2007037164

1 2 3 4 5 / 11 12 10 09 08

CONTENTS

108 POEMS

FOREWORD

I met Ko Un in Seoul in 1989 at a poetry reading. A pre-
cocious scholar, then conscripted People's Army worker,
then alms begging monk ten years, then Buddhist News-
paper Editor-in-Chief, then published poet, then temple
Head Priest, then he took off his robes in nihilist despair.
Then he became headmaster of a southern Island charity
school, then prolific writer and drunk, then would-be sui-
cide, then militant nationalist rebel against police state,
then Secy. General of Association of Artists for Practical
Freedom, then detainee & political jailbird, meanwhile
prolific writer, translator, and literary archivist, then at age
50 a husband and father, then epic-historical militant bard,
prisoner in 1980, then epic poet of *Paekdu Mountain* and
narrative poet of character vignettes *Ten Thousand Lives*,
a monumental series of anecdotal "characters" written in
Korean spoken idiom, finally a demon-driven Bodhisattva
of Korean poetry, exuberant, demotic, abundant, obsessed

with poetic creation, "widely acknowledged to be Korea's foremost contemporary poet," according to his translators.

Familiar with some of his earlier poems in translations, especially some of the later trickster-like naturalistic life sketches of *Ten Thousand Lives*—tender portraits, humane, paradoxical, "ordinary" stories with hilarious twists & endings, a little parallel to the "Characters" of W. C. Williams and Charles Reznikoff, I was stopped short by the present volume.* 108 (count of beads in Buddhist mala) thought-stopping Koan-like mental firecrackers. I haven't gone thru Zen Practice, my lineage is Tibetan Kagyu, just sitting; and Gelugpa, some analytical meditation. But everyone eastern-literate knows the taste of Koan & Haiku & gatha & doha nonconceptual riddles—or conceptions that annul Conceptual speculation.

Ko Un backtracks from earlier "Crazy Wisdom" narratives & here presents what I take to be Zen mini-poems. I can't account for them, only half understand their implications and am attracted by the nubbin of poetry they present. Hard nuts to crack—yet many seem immediately nutty & empty at the same time: "before your mom / your burbling / was there" i.e., chortling you had before you were born.

---

* *The Sound of My Waves: Selected Poems by Ko Un*, translated by Brother Anthony of Taizé and Young-Moo Kim (Ithaca, NY: Cornell East Asia Series, 1993).

These poems are reminiscent of Ikkyu's manifestation of *shunyata*: "Oh yes things exist, like the echo of your voice when you yell at the foot of a huge mountain." Ko Un notices while "Walking Down a Mountain," "The autumn breeze tosses and turns lifeless / like a cast-off snakeskin."

The luminous broad humor's apparent: "A Drunkard ... staggering zigzag along. / sixty trillion cells, all drunk!"

Ko Un's imagination roves: "In a Tiny Prison Cell," "Italy today / Spain tomorrow / travel around a bit / Sri Lanka the day after."

And we have Classic ordinary mind (& speech & body): "Once you've had your shit, / wipe yourself and get out of here."

Or on Samsara, a "Mosquito": "Why, I'm really alive. / Scratch scratch."

A little Blakean empathy: "The worm dribbled a cry."

And a sense of quick transience: "That dog that'll die tomorrow / doesn't know it's going to die / It's barking fiercely."

Ko Un is a magnificent poet, a combination of Buddhist cognoscente, passionate political libertarian, and naturalist historian. This little book of Seon (Zen) poems gives a glimpse.

—ALLEN GINSBERG
· AUGUST 27, 1994

INTRODUCTION

In 1995, the poet Ko Un interviewed me for a program on the Buddhist television network in Seoul. As we sat together in the studio, sharing our thoughts and experiences on many topics, I felt I was in the presence of a Dharma brother. I told him I had the feeling we had done this many times before. The more I learned about his life, the closer I felt to him. Ko Un was a Buddhist monk, and he is also a poet, a writer, and an ardent worker for peace. He is also a man of great insight. When he was imprisoned by the military dictatorship for his efforts for peace, his deep Buddhist practice sustained him. Living mindfully in each moment, he knew what to do and what not to do to help himself and others as well.

When I was staying in the hills above Seoul, I was deeply moved by the spring magnolia flowers just outside my door. I entered the present moment deeply, and

I said to them, "Magnolia flowers, I know you are there, and that makes me very happy." I hope you will enjoy these poems in the same way. As you read Ko Un's poems, allow the poet in you to hear his voice. His poems are vivid, imaginative, and filled with light. Enter deeply into the present moment, reflect on each word, and meet the poet Ko Un face to face.

—THICH NHAT HANH
Plum Village, France
JULY 1997

POET'S WELCOME

The world renewed! I want to give water to every person journeying in search of a new world; I want to quench their weary bodies' thirst. I have to thaw out their frozen bodies with a blazing fire on cold evenings.

More than that, I long to give them strong bars of iron to hold on to, to prevent them from being swept away by raging storms.

People made of mud cannot cross streams, people made of wood cannot go near a fire. And surely even someone made of hard iron will rust away into so much junk in less than a century.

Here stands a good-for-nothing who let himself get soaked till the mud dissolved, set fire to himself so the wood disappeared, and the iron finally rusted away in the wind and the rain.

Go now. A new life has been born, and isn't that a new world?

The Buddhist meditative tradition, known as *Seon* in Korean, *Zen* in Japanese, *Chan* in Chinese, *dhyana* in Sanskrit, comes alive by first denying speech and writing.

A thrilling exercise, indeed! But this kind of denial is a realistic reflection of the backgrounds to the practice of Seon. Initially, the philosophies of Lao Tzu and Chuang Tzu served as background to the introduction of Seon into China from India. Early Chinese Buddhism prematurely hardened into a grand metaphysics of the upper classes. It was easily adopted as an elite form of speech and writing.

Seon appeared as a means of shattering the acts of speaking and writing, a powerful grassroots movement of rejection.

As a result, Seon made those who knew how to write reject writing completely, and was much more accessible to people who could not express themselves in words.

Moreover, Seon escaped from the religious system centered on monks and began to contribute to the legitimization of the ways of living of ordinary, common people and even of slaves. The Third Patriarch, Sengcan, and the Sixth, Huineng, were especially active in this direction.

Seon is mind and nothing else. Only through the true self within the mind can we meet a radically new world, one totally different from the old; that is the goal of Seon.

Seon sets out to come to the truth of all things by the rejection of all things and yet, despite this negating approach, the freewheeling Seon questions and answers came into being, as well as Seon poetry. By the eighth century, Seon had already given rise to the first age of Seon literature.

Seon literature is an intense act of the mind liberated from the established systems of speech and writing, a new and completely unfamiliar leap. The vitality of this unfamiliar state is the heart of Seon poetry.

Perhaps all poems are in fact Seon poems, in that this kind of vitality is inevitably found in every kind of poetry, even works not usually termed Seon poems, in their fascinating Seon-like tensions, urgency, and bald ellipses. Even the Japanese *haiku* is not unrelated to Seon poetry, insofar as each line crystallizes a precise insight into aspects of the human mind and of things.

Buddhist canonical writings can be classified into roughly twelve categories according to their literary types. Among them we find the *gatha*, which are truly poetic works, and *geyya*, where something that has first been expressed in prose is given added force by the use of verse. Here we may find the origins of Seon poetry.

Seon poetry enjoyed its initial Golden Age high in the mountains of Tang China (618–907) and its history has continued for more than a thousand years down to the present day.

Seon has preserved its own characteristics, and become one with poetry alone, never accepting the lengthy narratives and descriptions found in other forms of writing. That explains why Seon masters are poets, but never novelists.

Through ten years' experience of Seon life as a monk I gained a tiny scrap of experience of Seon poetry. In my thirty-five years as a poet, I've also become familiar with poetry's need to create its own tradition. Consequently, this collection of Seon poems is an act of poetry writing, not so much faithful to the history of Seon poetry as trying to get away from it.

I too need to encounter water, fire, and iron, because my ceaseless dream and desire is for a new world. Surely Seon is nothing other than a love for that world, just as a mother always knows what her kids are up to, and kids are always looking for their mother.

What?

—KO UN
JULY 30, 1993
and MAY 9, 2006

108 POEMS

ECHO

To mountains at dusk:
What are you?

What are you are you . . .

THE OWL

Midday owl
eyes glaring
can't see a thing.
Just wait.
Your night's sure to come.

BABY

Before you were born
before your dad
before your mom

your burbling
                        was there.

BLIND ANIRUDDHA

This man sank so deep into meditation
he lost his sight for good
but heaven's eyes opened.
He sees all that exists.

BEEF

Everything turns into something.
The most disheartening of moments.
    Cut it off.

Everything turns into something
while cows are turning into beef.

WALKING DOWN A MOUNTAIN

Looking back
    Hey!
There's no trace of the mountain I've just come down.
Where am I?
The autumn breeze tosses and turns lifeless
    like a cast-off snakeskin.

THREE NAMES

They're playing with Seon like children.
It's white! It's black! They quarrel.
Let's call it quits.
Then
they get up, dusting themselves off.

Once
for no reason
Chusa gave Baekpa
three separate names and said
If fine enough fellows appear
    later
allocate one of these to each of them
    Seokjeon
    Manam
    Daryun
Seokjeon went to the then-obscure Pak Han-yeong
Manam to Song Jong-heon
then came the monk Daryun.

One name
Manam
now hangs framed in Baegyang Temple
where at midnight the night bird sings.

BUSHMEN

For African bushmen
a dozen words are enough
for a whole Lifetime.

Oh true Father, Son and Holy Spirit.
Bushmen!

TESTING

Come here.

No feet.

I'm sending a bitch.
It'll bite your feet.

You son of a bitch!

Come tomorrow.

Tomorrow? What's tomorrow?

You son of a bitch!

BEYOND

Without you,
how can I possibly live?

DEEP FEELINGS

Waiting decades for one snowflake
my body glowed like charcoal
then went out.

With it, a sound of cicadas singing
was there, then wasn't.

koun

THE MONK GYEONGHO

You wouldn't be you
if you didn't know all about wine and women.
Only you didn't know about the rest
so a couple of ancient magpies
have built their nest on your head.

BROAD DAYLIGHT

A dry turd
with no flies around.

Is this Paradise? No.

A SMILE [1]

Standing in front of the smile
on the face of a boiled pig's head

by all means be as generous.

CLOTHES

King Ashoka brought a suit of clothes
Manjushri hid away.
No help for it.
King Ashoka went back home
and put the suit on.
Then he perceived that "river is river."

A DRUNKARD

I've never been an individual entity.
Sixty trillion cells!
I'm a living collectivity.
I'm staggering zigzag along,
sixty trillion cells, all drunk!

THE LOTUS SUTRA

The Lotus Sutra. Ultimate reality.
So far
you've been bashing me badly.
Now
I'll cudgel you, bastard.
Oh! Ouch!
You're made for bashing.
Oh! Ouch!
Oh! Ouch!

The Lotus Sutra dashed away.
    Fields open wide,
      once the farmers have gone.

SITTING

If you sit, you'll kill Buddha, kill mother.
Don't sit.
Don't stand.
All five oceans six continents
     even
that cinnamon tree in the bright moonlight
here and there are all a scalding cauldron lid.
Nowhere to put your feet down.
What's to be done?

AN ALLEY

A blind alley. I turn back.
  Great.
Here and there
bright lights

Up an alley in hill-girded Jeongneung.

MOON AT MIDDAY

Sun-face Buddha is eighteen hundred years old
Moon-face Buddha one single night
Sun-face Moon-face are said to be not two but one.
If that's true,
moon, rise
after sunset.

Just look at that daytime moon up there.
Sheer ignorance!

A TEMPLE'S MAIN HALL

A big mistake!

Much better
to turn back at the front gate.

THE MASTER'S SCROLL

The monk Dahui of ancient Sung
set fire to his master's scroll
        of the Blue Cliff Records.
Well done. He did well.

Yet here's the work in question.

A RAINBOW

There are such things. I straighten myself.

SOUTH AND NORTH

The head monk of Bohyeon Temple
up in Myohyang Mountain dialed
and the head monk of Daeheung Temple
down in Haenam took the call.
How are you getting on these days?
Our Buddha's turned round.
Ours has turned round too.

Not only there.
North and South, every Buddha had turned round.

What fine fellows.

MEDITATION ROOM

Try sitting
    not just for one kalpa
but for ten kalpas.
No enlightenment will come.

Simply play for a while with agonies, illusions,
        then stand up.

LATE SUMMER

Into water. Splash!
Into flames.
Eek, hot!

While summer goes bouncing on,
fruit ripens beyond.

A SUDDEN SHOWER

Several billion buddhas pouring down.
The brook busy babbling.
In addition
to the buddha corpses
other corpses are floating down too.
Real cool.

IDLE TALK

Dharma's father, Huike.
Shenxiu and Huineng, Hongren's fathers.
Shenxiu had fun in the palace.
Huineng had so many fathers
that the whole southern region got dizzy.

A really immoral family!

A FRIEND

Hey! With the clay you dug out
I fashioned a buddha.
It rained.
The buddha turned back into clay.

Pointless as the clear skies after rain.

BAR BY A ROAD JUNCTION

Awake?
If awake, joy,
sorrow nowhere.
Looking out after downing three cups of liquor
in an inn by a road junction,
that's what I heard the rain-swept road say.

KoUn

GLEANING

A patriarch's sayings are just
ears of grain in a field
and this year of poor harvest
with them . . .

DAYFLY

Three hundred-millionths of a second.
If that's how long one particle lasts
think how endless one day is.
You say a day's too short?
You greedy thing.

A PHANTOM

Deer can grow long horns!
Now the idle wind has got caught on their horns
and can't budge an inch.

Hey you, walking across the hillside!

A ROSARY

Angulimala was a devil of a cutthroat.
That fellow
sliced off the fingers of the people he killed
and wore them
strung dingle-dangle around his neck,
including his father's fingers.

That was a real hundred-eight bead rosary.
Every bead on the string
a life.

MOON [1]

The bow taut.
Twang!
The arrow strikes

　　　　　　your eye.

By the pain of your darkness the moon rose.

ONE WORD

Too quick! Too quick!
You call a stick of firewood
fire. Dear me!

LEPERS

Nonsense is not only eighty-four
thousand sutras but
Oh! sounds,
Gosh! sounds,
all nonsense.
Pull out Bodhidharma's eyebrows.
Pull out the Sixth Patriarch's toenails.

Ah, some lepers are playing their pipes over there.

MASTER BOJO OF GORYEO

One fellow stood on his head
did yoga till he died.
Another one
piled up wood that he set alight
then climbed on top
became a "Lotus in Flames."

Master Bojo of Goryeo
took his place on the podium
gave a hundred answers to a hundred questions
then got down from the podium
and sat on the floor . . .

Green leaves turn red then die.
Oh no, stop all that.

A GREEN FROG [1]

One green frog.
As you croak
black clouds are filling the sky.

The strongest guy in the world,
you squirt.

IN YOUR BOSOM

A century in your bosom.
No nation
No friends
No way for me to take.

What rapture, the ground of darkness.

CUCKOO

At dawn three cuckoos sit side by side.
Not a word about
>How fine this world!
>How fine that world!
Yesterday's cuckoo-cuckoo quite forgotten.
Too early yet for today's cuckoo-cuckoo.
The best time of day!

A SMILE [II]

Shakyamuni held up a lotus
so Kashyapa smiled.
Not at all.
The lotus smiled
so Kashyapa smiled.

Nowhere was Shakyamuni!

THE HORIZON

I stood facing the horizon over the East Sea.
What had become of the seventeen hundred
koan-riddles?
    The sound of waves
    the sound of waves.
Playing with you I threw them away.

MOUNTAIN IS MOUNTAIN

"Mountain is mountain
water is water," Daineng chanted.
"Mountain is not mountain
water is not water," Daineng chanted.
Eat your food.
Once you've eaten, go shit.

MOUNTAINTOP

What do you say there is up on the mountaintop?
Come down.
A peachtree's flowering at the crossroads.
"I'm off walking again today . . ."

FARAWAY LIGHTS

Traveling by night
distant lights were my strength.
By them alone
by them alone
my yesterday today and tomorrow too.

RIPPLES [I]

Look! Do all the ripples move
because one ripple starts to move?
        No.
It's just that all the ripples move at once.

Everything's gone greatly askew from the start.

ASKING THE WAY

You blockheads who ask what buddha is.
Ask now about every living being instead.
Ask about all living things.
When you're hungry
    ask about food.
Ask the moonlight about the way.
Find a port where lemon trees bloom
    where lemon trees bloom.
Ask about places to drink in the port.

Ask and ask till nothing's left to ask.

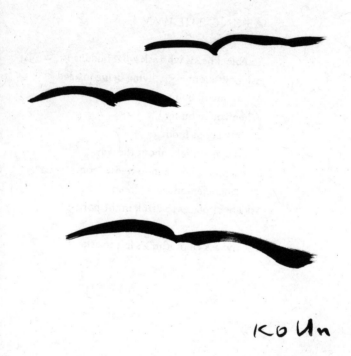

Ko Un

BABY MAGPIES

You idiot. Don't you know?
Shakyamuni's dad was a demon,
     not King Suddhodana.

Unskilled chatter of baby magpies at dawn. How lovely.

BLUE SKIES

Hey, man, cry your eyes out.

IN A TINY PRISON CELL

If all the nations aren't in here
where are the fine
fluttering flags of every country?
Italy today
Spain tomorrow
    travel around a bit
Sri Lanka the day after.

A LION

The lion's in the cave!
    Lurks
The lion's out of the cave!
    Looks
The lion's at the edge of the cave!
    Looms
The lion's run away!
    Limps

Is this kind of debate a proper job
for a grasshopper?

THE PATH

Take this path. It leads to Nirvana.

Excuse me.
I'll follow my own path.
Over rocky crags or under water.

That's the old master's path, the corpse's path.

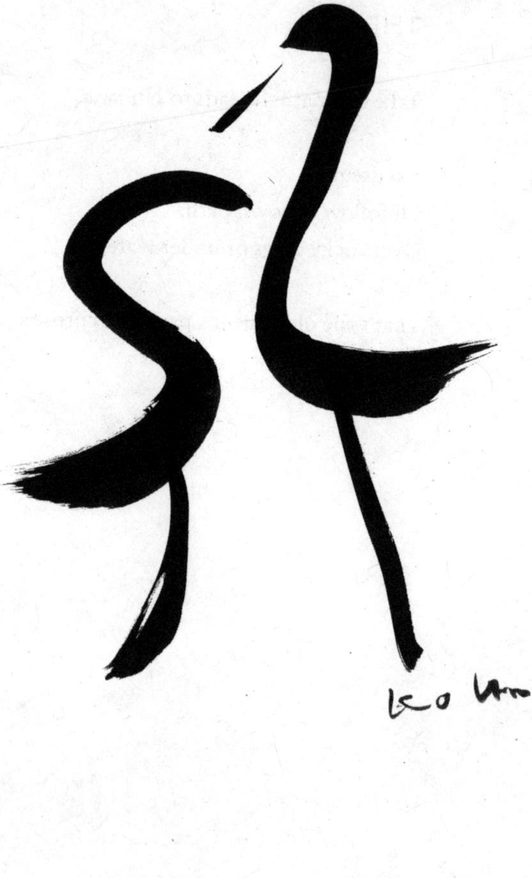

A CERTAIN BIRD

One kind of bird eats up its mother.

The mother hatching and feeding her chick
is feeding her own death.
Like mother like chick.
Eating up mother
is the natural thing for mother and chick.

THE WASH

The wash flaps, a bodhisattva not
knowing it's a bodhisattva.

PALGONG MOUNTAIN

Jails are crammed full of great masters.
Killer-and-thief, thief-and-killer,
would-be killer-thief and all the rest.

To ensure Daegu jail's crammed full
every temple on Palgong Mountain
is without great masters,
even those imitating great masters,
as wind bells tinkle.

THE WIND

Never beg the wind for mercy.
Tall wild lilies and such
scented white lilies and such
one-day lilies and such
once all your stems have snapped
produce new buds. It's not too late.

ONE DAY

Lightning over the hill in front
thunder over the hill behind
between the two
    one dumb pebble.

SIMPLY

We're each going our own way
but we say
it's because someone told us to.
The water simply flows down the hills
but we say
it's because someone told it to.
Human wisdom's pitiful stuff.

STEAK

Drinking in downtown Daejeon
my mouth was stuffed full
with a big lump of broiled steak
but suddenly I couldn't swallow it
    couldn't spit it out . . .
outside the pouring rain was shouting:
Quick! Say something!

What?

IN DAYLIGHT

After the rain, the waters rose every-
where.
Twelve no thirfourfifsixteen swallows
are soaring high.

JONGNO STREET

As I went strolling down Jongno Street in Daegu
    I bought and drank a bottle of schnapps.

OLD BUDDHA

Hey, what were you saying about old Buddha?
Why, old Buddha's no Buddha.
Real Buddha's a fish just netted
    leaping and jumping.

REEDS IN JEJU ISLAND

Early November. Jeju reed fields are
white with tufted reeds.
A scarecrow's set in the middle.

It's watching the sea. The sea's watching it.

kolln

A STONE BETWEEN TWO FIELDS

Aha, real Buddha's out of doors.
The future world
should be opening like this:
    no distinction between inside and out.

And all the long long day
    cuckoos chant prayers.

MOON [II]

What's that you say? We have to look at the moon
and forget the finger pointing at the moon?
    You blockhead!

Do what you like. Forget them both, or not.

ODAE MOUNTAIN

Mount Odae clapped
so Mount Ami laughed.

Where's that, Mount Ami?
Question asked after half-a-day's nap.

SPRING DREAMS

The night before last I beat up Hanshan in a dream.
Last night I embraced Chunhyang in a dream.
Yesterday I received twenty phone calls.
Today I bought ten strong nails
after watching a Chinese movie
    at Gwangsin Cinema in Anseong.
Back home I hammered in the nails and hung up photos.

Hanshan and Chunhyang in photos! I'm so happy.

A GREEN FROG [II]

My master's not Hyobong the monk.
It's a green frog's ten years
stuck motionless
at the end of a pole.

RIPPLES [II]

Stoop lower and lower
till you're nearly touching the ripples.

There's the bodhisattva Manjushri.

HEAVY RAIN

Rain pouring down all day long
not a beast anywhere in sight.
Alright!
You guys! Come out!
    Come out and play in the rain.

The sky will come out tomorrow and the
day after tomorrow.

WEAKLINGS

If there are great men
interestingly enough
there are weaklings too.
Who are these fellows
who lack an ordinary heart?

The monk Nanquan used to go on about
how the ordinary heart really is the Dao.

WIND

A wind stirs.
Ah, this world, that world.

LEAVING HOME

If leaving home is what a monk's job involves,
then coming home
    really
    really
is what a buddha's job is.

But surely you can only really come home
        if you've really left home, can't you?

A HERMIT

Jang Gu-Seong the hermit was busy shitting
when he heard frogs croaking. It made him recite:

The croaking of frogs on moonlit nights in early spring
pierces the world from end to end, makes all one family.

Once you've had your shit,
    wipe yourself and get out of here.

WORDS I LIKE

I'd rather sink to the bottom of the sea
    till the end of time
than seek liberation from a lot of sages.

Great! I've got wine in my glass
    and this saying of Master Stonehead's too.

MOSQUITO

I've been bitten by a mosquito.
Thanks a million.
Why, I'm really alive.
    Scratch scratch.

HANSHAN AND SHIDE

Don't go serving those fools
    Hanshan and Shide
like other people do.
Today I plan to run to Tiantai Mountain,
pull it all down and
plant opium poppies where it stood.
Yes, red opium poppies, flowers.

THE WOMEN OF MAJEONG

The women of Majeong village
the old women
once all the girls had left the place
those old women
would help each other
in furrowed fields under a scorching sun.
Out weeding they'd stop work
to dance a merry dance
singing "Come back to Busan harbor"
dancing a merry dance.

A NEW WAY

Now go sinking into the sea.
To the whales, the sharks and the shrimps,
all the way down to the darkest deep.
There you'll have many companions!

Don't go treading in Buddha's footsteps
        nothing like that
just sink into the sea.

HOUSE

Grow high. The devil can't find you.
Grow deep. Buddha can't find you.
Build a house and live there.
Gourd creepers will climb over it,
their flowers dazzling at midnight.

A SINGLE WORD

Too late.

The world had already heard
    my word
before I spoke it.
The worm had heard.
The worm dribbled a cry.

A SHOOTING STAR

Wow! You recognize me.

Ko Un

SUMMER

The sightless sunflower follows the sun.
The sightless moonflower blossoms in moonlight.
    Foolishness.
That's all they know.
Dragonflies fly by day
              beetles by night.

AN AUTUMN NIGHT

Daddy
Daddy

A cricket sings.

TODAY

Ha ha! Today's the best day. The best
for some guy to kick the bucket
and for some other guy to get born,
for life-starting cries, for tavern songs.

The sky's clouded over.

EARTHWORM

The earthworm wriggles onwards.
    Wriggles on then rests.
The sky's good friend.

A BOWL OF ROWAN TEA

Here's a bowl of rowan tea. Drink up.
Rather than sing about thousands of miles
    travel two or three.

Hey, you tongues.

ONE LITTLE KID

I refuse to devote myself to the Three Jewels.
As I was walking along
I met a little kid
got fascinated by its innocence.
How useless are candles, incense and things.
Oh dear! I've missed that dragonfly.

SLAMMING THE DOOR

Go away. I'm not in.
Go and look
at the bottom of the sea.
Here's only a stray dog that shits
    then licks its dirt.

Yeuh!

FRIENDS

Hello there!
the shout rang out.
Cape Guryong here!
Over the sea Dodong, Ulleung Island.
What's up?
Come across for a while.
Sure, I'll be right over.

The night waves were roaring
the lamplight was bright in one pub on
Cape Guryong.

LATE ONE NIGHT

Late one night a fox changes its shape
and slips into your room as a pretty girl:
  what will you do?

Don't be stupid. I'll grab her.

Ha ha, you fox's husband, you.
A fox is more fun than Buddha, of course.

  You bet.

WHY KILL?

Let it be. Please, let it be.
Kill Buddha
if you meet him?
Kill mother and father
if you meet them? Why kill?
Things made of clay all fall to bits
once soaked by monsoon rains.

BIRTHPLACE

Don't ask Chunseong the monk about his Master.
He'll say: "Han Yong-Un? Never heard of him."
Don't ask Chunseong the monk where he came from.
If he's asked where he was born
he says

My mother's c-nt.

A ceremonial robe draped
over his naked body
he sat in meditation.
Under this belly
that's my mother's son's pr-ck.

Greece and Rome find it funny, no reason.

A MOONLIT NIGHT

Everything out here's shining bright.
The mortar's bright and empty.

No wonder the grasshoppers are silent!

A MOONLESS NIGHT

No moon up
yet the two hundred miles
between you and me
shine bright all the night long.
That dog that'll die tomorrow
    doesn't know it's going to die.
It's barking fiercely.

A NAP

All the world is in the womb.
I've had a good sleep.
How about going out now?

To mewl, at best.

ONE FLY

The fly settled.
I squashed it with my palm.
      No more fly.
What's going on here?
You must be stupid.
What's going on here?

WILD BOARS

A group of wild boars
dug into the Golden Mountain.
As they dug deeper
the gold became more dazzling.

Accept my respects, uncle boars.

HARSH TRAINING

My, you're cooking a meal of sand!
Who's going to eat that?

Out in the fields the cereals are ripe.

Why, you are less than even the sparrows!
Ugh! Ouch!

TRIPITAKA KOREANA

Finding the way blocked by utter gibberish
I turned back
and saw
a snake.

Snakes know the ways of snakes so well.

ANANDA

Even Shakyamuni could never tame Ananda
but Kashyapa kicked him out and tamed him.
Throw away all you know.
Throw away all you don't know.
Then and only then one star shines bright.

THE POLE STAR

If you vanished
the north would vanish
the south would vanish
east and west would vanish.
    No.

RECORDS OF THE
LAMP TRANSMISSION

Why did they keep the transmission secret?
Sons of bitches!
Bow-wow-wow!

On moonlit nights everything's out in the open.

A LETTER

Seon Master Hanam's reply
to a letter from Seon Master Gyeongbong

was one blank sheet of paper.

Ha ha, they're cousins, not uncles.

YEFU

Old Yefu took his shit
smeared it on the walls of his cell.
Monks burned up Yefu's Song in the Diamond Sutra
claiming he was senile.

This tale's one part of Yefu's Song . . .
Look closely, look.

PIG

Before you there's no bandit called Shakyamuni
behind you there's no beggar called Maitreya

That was before your snout started to grunt.

Ko Un

PARTING

Farewell.
Fare well.

NOTES ON THE POEMS

ECHO (page 21)
The one-word question "Mweo-nya? What?" is one of the most funda-
mental challenges in the Korean Seon tradition.

BLIND ANIRUDDHA (page 24)
Aniruddha was a member of the family of Shakyamuni and a contem-
porary of the historical Buddha; there are tales of how he would always
fall asleep while the Master taught but later studied deeply and so at
last attained enlightenment.

THREE NAMES (page 28)
Chusa was the pen name of Kim Jong-Hui (1786–1856), famous for his
calligraphy. The other names are monks, of whom the "obscure" Pak
Han-yeong is the most famous since he was the friend of some of the
greatest early modern Korean poets in the Independence Movement,
and the teacher of the poet Seo Jeong-Ju (Midang). Baegyang Temple is
in South Jeolla Province.

TESTING (page 31)
The title of this poem is a word used in Seon to designate a form of
dialogue in which a master tests the extent to which a disciple has ad-
vanced in understanding.

THE MONK GYEONGHO (page 35)

Gyeongho (1846–1912) entered a monastery when he was nine, began to study sutras at fourteen, and taught at twenty-three. When he was fifty-nine, he suddenly disappeared, then re-appeared with a new name. He practiced a controversial Way that included breaking precepts.

CLOTHES (page 38)

King Ashoka (c.264–c.226), having unified India, made Buddhism its official religion and launched a vast program of buildings for which he inaugurated Buddhist art. Manjushri is the name of the bodhisattva of wisdom and intellect. "River is river" is an echo of a famous Chinese Seon story about Taineng (see the poem "Mountain Is Mountain" on page 69).

THE LOTUS SUTRA (page 40)

The Lotus Sutra is one of the most important works in the Buddhist canon but Seon tends to deny the importance of written teachings in favor of direct personal experience.

SITTING (page 41)

Sitting is the standard expression for "doing Seon meditation" since it traditionally involves sitting for long periods of time. The challenge to "kill Buddha" and "kill parents" is part of the Buddhist search for detachment from all bonds.

AN ALLEY (page 42)

Jeongneung was until recently an isolated, hill-girt village to the north of Seoul.

THE MASTER'S SCROLL (page 45)

The "Blue Cliff Records" were compiled between 1111 and 1117 by the Chinese Chan master Yuanwu Keqin.

SOUTH AND NORTH (page 47)

Myohyang Mountain is in North Korea, Haenam is in the southern-most part of South Jeolla Province; temples in the two places are made the setting for an evocation of the total division of the two parts of

Korea, between which telephone conversations are not permitted. The statues have each turned to face the other half of Korea.

MEDITATION ROOM (page 48)
A kalpa is the number of years it takes for heaven and earth to pass through one complete cycle of abolition and renewal, the largest conceivable unit of time.

IDLE TALK (page 51)
The names mentioned here are those of some of the Six Patriarchs, great masters of the Chinese Chan schools; Bodhidharma was an Indian, the legendary First Patriarch, perhaps active in China between 470 and 570. Huineng (638–713) is the Sixth. In this poem the hierarchy of master and disciple is deliberately confused. The story of how Hongren, the Fifth Patriarch, chose the temple's kitchen-boy Huineng to be his successor rather than Shenxiu, who was its chief monk, is found in the "Liu zu tanjing" composed in about 820.

A ROSARY (page 59)
Angulimala is reputed to have lived in the days of the historical Buddha. He was said to have killed over ninety people and to have promised that his hundredth victim would be his own mother.

LEPERS (page 62)
On Bodhidharma see the note to "Idle Talk" above. In Chinese art, he is represented with eyebrows reaching to the ground.

MASTER BOJO OF GORYEO (page 63)
Bojo is a name given posthumously to the Korean Seon master Jinul, who founded Songgwang Temple in South Jeolla Province. Goryeo is the name given to the period of Korean history between 918 and 1392; it also designated the country itself.

A SMILE II (page 67)
A famous story tells how Shakyamuni silently held up a lotus flower; the other disciples were puzzled but Kashyapa (Mahakashyapa) smiled, showing that he had understood the implied wordless message. This is seen as the beginning of the Seon tradition.

THE HORIZON (page 68)
The kind of paradoxical riddle-question used in Seon is usually called a "koan" in English, from the Japanese pronunciation of the Chinese characters.

MOUNTAIN IS MOUNTAIN (page 69)
See note to "Clothes" (page 141).

BABY MAGPIES (page 75)
King Suddhodana is the name given to the father of the historical Buddha Shakyamuni in the traditional tales.

PALGONG MOUNTAIN (page 83)
Palgong Mountain is near Daegu, in the southeastern part of Korea.

MOON II (page 94)
When they want to distinguish between essence and means, Korean masters often refer to a traditional saying: "The finger pointing at the moon is not the moon."

SPRING DREAMS (page 96)
Hanshan was a famous monk poet of ancient China, also known in English by the translation of his name, Cold Mountain. Chunhyang is the heroine of Korea's most popular ancient love story.

RIPPLES II (page 98)
Manjushri is the name of the bodhisattva of wisdom and intellect.

WEAKLINGS (page 100)
Nanquan (748–834) was a Chinese monk.

WORDS I LIKE (page 104)
The name "Master Stonehead" is quite common among monks in both China and Korea. This poem quotes words by the Chinese monk Shitou (700–790).

HANSHAN AND SHIDE (page 106)
These two are commonly depicted in a popular Chinese porcelain sculpture as two fat men rolling with laughter. There are several legends about their encounter on the Chinese mountain where Hanshan was a hermit.

ONE LITTLE KID (page 118)
The Three Jewels (triratna) of Buddhism are the Buddha, the Dharma (teaching), and the Sangha (community).

FRIENDS (page 120)
Cape Guryong is on the east coast of Korea, and Ulleung Island some miles off it.

WHY KILL? (page 122)
In the disciplines of Buddhism, the call to break all ties with the world of phenomena is sometimes dramatized in such expressions as "kill Buddha if you meet him" or "kill your parents if you meet them."

BIRTHPLACE (page 123)
Han Yong-Un (Manhae) (1879–1944) was a noted Buddhist monk, a poet and novelist. He was one of the original signatories of the Declaration of Korean Independence of March 1, 1919.

TRIPITAKA KOREANA (page 130)
This is the name given to the huge collection of Buddhist scriptures carved on over eighty thousand wooden blocks in the thirteenth century and now preserved at the temple Haeinsa in central South Korea.

ANANDA (page 131)
Ananda and Kashyapa are both mentioned in the oldest stories about the life of the historical Buddha, Shakyamuni, as being particularly close to the Master.

RECORDS OF THE LAMP TRANSMISSION (page 134)
This is the title of a Chinese treatise on meditation, the "Jingde chuandeng lu," written by Daoyuan in the Song dynasty.

YEFU (page 136)
The Diamond Sutra is one of the major Mahayana sutras. Its full name is the Diamond-cutter Perfection of Wisdom Sutra or the Vajracchedika and it is a short version, made in the fourth century, of earlier Prajñaparamita (Perfection of Wisdom) Sutras, central to the Madhyamaka (Middle Way) school of philosophical Buddhism.

One part of the Diamond Sutra is entitled "Yefu's Song," and the poem plays on the fact that there was a Chinese monk of that name, whose life history the poem evokes, in the eleventh century (fl. 1063).

BIOGRAPHY OF KO UN:
A TRAVELER ON THE WAY

*"I did not come to this world to play.
As birds sing, I came to this world to sing,
keep silent, and to work."*—Ko Un

Ko Un was born August 1, 1933, the first son of a farmer in a small village in North Jeolla Province. He was a sickly infant, and at times it seemed doubtful whether he would survive. But he did. As a young boy, he studied Chinese classics and learned to read and write Korean from a neighbor's servant. (Under Japanese colonialism, it was prohibited to teach Korean in schools.) He entered primary school at age ten, and when Korea was liberated from Japanese rule, he was the only student in his class who knew how to read and write Korean. Ko Un was also talented in painting. One day he placed a note on his wall that said, "There is no one but van Gogh." It was his dream to become a painter.

In 1949, a year before the Korean War, Ko Un found a book of poems along the roadside by Han Ha-Wun, the beloved Korean leper-poet. He spent the whole night reading and weeping. Han Ha-Wun had deeply affected him, and he decided to become a poet. He wandered the streets doing whatever work he could to make a living, and finally he was hired to teach Korean and art.

The 1950–1953 war had a deep effect on Ko Un. He witnessed unspeakable violence by the Communists— rape, murder, suicide, brothers killing brothers. When the Korean army regained the country, they killed anyone who had participated in the Communist regime, including Ko Un's family members, neighbors, friends, relatives, and his first love. Ko Un was given the order to transport corpses, and he carried them on his back for many nights. Overwhelmed by the suffering, Ko Un roamed the hills and mountains, and many thought he had gone insane. He finally quit his job as a teacher and began working as a clerk for the American Navy. It was during that time that he heard about the monk Hyecho and determined to meet him.

Hyecho was the son of Park Je-Seon, one of the five officials who turned Korea over to Japan at the end of the Li dynasty. Hyecho's shame at this drove him to become a monk. In 1952, at age nineteen, Ko Un became a novice monk under Hyecho's guidance. He was given the Buddhist name Chungchang and the *gongan*, "All the dharmas return to the one. Where does the one return?"* But within a year Hyecho fell in love and left the monkhood. Ko Un's shock was so great he attempted suicide.

Ko Un wandered as a begging monk for a year. Finally, exhausted, he went to see Master Hyobong, and received the gongan Mu (literally: "No," "Nothingness," "Emptiness"). Ko Un described his new master as "very kind and very strict." Hyobong Seonsa had previously been a lawyer and judge. Once he had to demand the death penalty, and he was so tormented that he left his family and became a disciple of Sokdu Seonsa.** When Hyobong arrived, Seokdu Seonsa asked him, "How many steps did you take to come here?" Hyobong circled the room, and Seokdu accepted him as his disciple.

One day, while washing rice in the monastery, Ko Un dropped a few grains. Hyobong Seonsa saw this and started crying at the waste of this precious food. Ko Un had the realization that the spiritual and material

---

* A meditation topic. Same as Japanese koan.

** Sokdu Seonsa was a Korean Seon master who practiced in the Diamond Mountains and was Hyobong Seonsa's teacher. He was known as a master who did not accept students freely.

are one from the very beginning. After that day, Ko Un never wasted one grain of rice. He even gathered rice that had been thrown into the ditch as refuse. Ko Un recollects, "Before I became a disciple of Hyobong Seonsa, I was very knowledgeable about Western philosophy, sutra study, and the teachings of the early Seon Patriarchs.* In fact, I was pedantic and enjoyed showing off. Seeing this, my master said, 'Be ignorant in everything. Let go of everything and only meditate on "Mu." Mu is your breath, your farts, and your father. Let go even of emptiness.' Free from words, I began to fly, and from this freedom, I met with language again."

Korea is a land of poetry. While young people in the West dream of being movie stars or athletes, Korean young people dream of becoming poets. Everyone, regardless of status, throughout Korean history has written poetry. Poetry and poets are revered in Korea and Ko Un aspired to be a poet. When he became editor of the *Buddhist Newspaper*, he wrote poems to fill all the empty spaces.

During the Japanese occupation, the quality of monks and nuns in Korea had declined, and Ko Un did

---

* Seon is the Korean pronunciation of the Sanskrit word dhyana, which means meditation, and is commonly known in English by its Japanese transliteration, "Zen."

his best to try to restore the Sangha, train monks, and educate laypeople. Ko Un practiced meditation traditionally, but he was also wild. One rainy day, he danced naked on the grounds of the Jogye Temple, and the other monks followed his example! Then, while studying Ashvaghosa's *The Awakening of Faith in the Mahayana*, Ko Un had a realization—that emptiness is not nihilistic, that to understand emptiness is to realize the oneness of all beings. This was a turning point in his life.

In 1959, Ko Un entered the beautiful Haeinsa, one of the three main Buddhist monasteries in Korea. One day while walking beside a stream, he found a human skull. He took it to his room and every night he talked to the skull:

Did you practice hard?

No, I wasted the whole day.

Ah, that's the problem.

What's the problem?

That you pretend to practice.

Oh, you skull Zen master!

Oh, you future skull Zen master!

In 1960, when Syngman Rhee's government was overthrown, Ko Un was at Haeinsa. The Rhee government had supported monks who were celibate, and now, the formerly excluded married monks gathered force and attempted to gain temples they had lost under the Rhee administration.* One day Ko Un was notified that some monks were approaching Haeinsa, accompanied by thugs. Everyone left the temple except Ko Un and a few young monks. Ko Un said, "It was not that I had courage, but I had to stay. We began to meditate. I wore the official robe and held the temple seal in my hand. When the married monks came, they couldn't do anything. Our meditation posture kept them from taking any action. But in the afternoon, they got the thugs drunk, and the gang members dragged me down by my arms and legs, tearing my robe and scraping my head on the stone steps. The monks asked me to transfer Haeinsa to them, and I shouted, 'Kill me now!' " Praised for saving Haeinsa, Ko Un was given the position of abbot. However, within a short time, he resigned, buried the skull, and accepted an abbotship at Jeondeung Temple on Ganghwa Island. There, he thought deeply about his future as a monk and poet.

In 1963, he published an essay announcing his return to secular life. He feared that if he tried to master both Seon and poetry at the same time he would lose both. So he chose one—literature. But the secular world did not receive Ko Un kindly.

---

* Traditionally, Buddhist monks are celibate. The Japanese changed that tradition in the nineteenth century, and during their occupation imposed marriage on Korean Buddhist monks.

He spent some of his time browsing in secondhand bookstores. In one store, he found a Japanese translation of Mikhail Sholokhov's novel, *And Quiet Flows the Don*, recounting the struggles of individuals living in the midst of the Russian Revolution. Ko Un read the book every night for seven days, deeply moved by its grief and suffering. The book led him to disparage his own work along with all of Korea's literary output for the previous half century. One night, he drank four bottles of liquor, collected all his works, and burned them. He felt it was not literature, compared with the work of Sholokhov.

After another failed suicide attempt, Ko Un lived on Jeju Island for four years, established a library and a public high school, and taught Korean and art to poor children. However, he continued to drink heavily and he suffered from insomnia. When he returned to Seoul, his insomnia continued, and he was tormented by a nihilism that affected many intellectuals after the Korean War. In 1970, Ko Un made his last suicide attempt. He was discovered by army reservists in a valley near Seoul and recovered consciousness after thirty hours. It was the beginning of a new life as an activist. During this period, Ko Un published many books of poetry and essays.

In the winter of 1970, Ko Un was spending the night at a tavern, and found an old newspaper on the floor with an article about a laborer's self-immolation. "Why did this young man have to die, while I am still alive?" he thought. The article pulled Ko Un out of the abyss and changed his life forever.

In the 1970s and 1980s, Ko Un was a leading political activist, protesting Korea's military dictatorship. He participated in the labor and unification movements and was regularly visited by the Korean CIA, and followed by policemen wherever he went. He was tortured and, as a result, lost his hearing. He now has an artificial eardrum. In 1980 he was imprisoned, together with many others, at the time of the tragic events known as the Gwangju Democratic Uprising, in which so many innocent lives were lost.[*] Ko Un was falsely accused of conspiring to incite civil war. In his dark cell, he realized the interconnectedness of all beings, and he resolved to create something to commemorate all the people he had known from Korean history and during his life. In 1982, aged forty-nine, he was released by a special pardon. The following year he married Lee Sang-Hwa, a professor of English literature. In 1985, their daughter, Cha Ryeong, was born.

"I was born because of literature, and because of litera-

---

[*] Military leader Chun Doo-Hwan had massacred many citizens of Kwangju, who had tried to begin a new era of democracy after the assassination of military dictator Park Chung-Hee.

ture I have a life that should have ended many times. Eventually my death will be literature itself. Literature has to reveal the highest truth and challenge all lies. I can only write in my native language. Even my prepositions are bloodstained blossoms that contain the life and history of all my ancestors." Many of Ko Un's literary works—more than one hundred volumes of poems, essays, critical reviews, and novels—spring from his practice of Zen. They either minimize language or free themselves from language. When Ko Un left the monastery, he left behind a corrupt organization, not Buddhism. His Zen Buddhism is always with him. He has said that, while in prison, it was Zen that sustained him.

Ko Un published his first book of poetry, *Other World Sensitivity*, in 1960, just after the April revolution that overthrew the Rhee government. From 1960 to 1967, Ko Un wrote mostly lyric poems, often focusing on death. From 1974 to 1983, he wrote passionate, untamed political poems. Since 1984, beginning with the publication of *Homeland Stars*, he has entered a new phase of affirmation. His work in process, conceived in prison, is *Ten Thousand Lives*, commemorating both historical and obscure personages.

In 1991, Ko Un completed a best-selling Buddhist novel *Hwa-eom-kyeong* (Garland Sutra), based on the

Avatamsaka Sutra, describing Sudhana's endless quest for truth.*

In Ko Un's early work, he sees emptiness without form; in his middle period as a passionate political activist, he sees form; in his later years, after the experience of solitary confinement and of being a husband and father, he sees form in emptiness and emptiness in form.

His current work focuses on themes of self and no-self, based on the teachings of Buddhism and the work of Laozi and Zhuangzi. He uses both Zen-like direct language and a vast epic style. He has recently published *Seon*, a novel in two volumes about important Zen masters since Bodhidharma, and an epic poem in seven volumes, *Baekdu Mountain*, describing the independence movement during the Japanese occupation of Korea.

What are Zen poems? You have to taste each poem. That is their beauty. Ko Un asks us to participate in the festivity of our lives and to move beyond our usual limits. That is one reason Zen masters sometimes use irreverent language to shock us beyond our usual restrictions.

It is my great joy to help bring you Ko Un, a truly compassionate poet, who said, "One must cry many days before becoming a poet." These 108 poems are not

---

* This novel was published in 2005 in English as *Little Pilgrim* by Parallax Press.

only 108 glimpses of Ko Un. They are also 108 chances to look at ourselves.

—OK-KOO KANG GROSJEAN

Berkeley, California
JUNE 1997

TRANSLATOR'S NOTE

When this volume first appeared in 1997, the publisher gave it the English title *Beyond Self* but no one was perfectly happy with it. It now receives a title more exactly reflecting the simple Mweo-nya of the original Korean, even if this change might confuse some into believing that it is a different book. Except for some revisions of the translations to bring them closer to the originals, this is the same volume.

The publication by Parallax Press of a volume of Korean Seon poems in translation was an exceptional event, very largely due to the untiring efforts of a remarkable woman, Ok-Koo Kang Grosjean. She was born in Korea but came to the United States in 1963, became known as a poet and translator, and was a great admirer of Ko Un. She died of cancer in October 2000, a few days before her sixtieth birthday. The words she wrote for the first edition are printed here virtually unchanged.*

Ok-Koo Kang Grosjean's biography of Ko Un ends virtually with the birth of his daughter in 1985. Since then Ko Un has lived quietly in Anseong, and published many volumes of poetry. The series *Maninbo* (*Ten Thousand Lives*) alone now counts some twenty-five volumes. Ko Un's work has become known across the world, with many translations being published in every major language. He himself has made countless journeys, visiting every continent and reading to large audiences with many of the most significant poets of today's world. In 2005, Parallax Press published Ko Un's great novel *Hwaeom-kyeong* in English as *Little Pilgrim*. At the same time, Green Integer Press published selections from the first ten volumes of *Maninbo* as *Ten Thousand Lives*. This was followed by Green Integer's edition of a large collection from all Ko Un's poetry, *Songs for Tomorrow*.

In this edition of *What?*, Korean names and words are printed according to the Revised Korean Romanization (RKR) system, where the short "o" sound heard in the English word "off" is indicated by "eo" and "eu" represents the "u" heard in "burn." The English-speak-

---

* One year later, in 2001 my fellow translator, Young-Moo Kim, also died of cancer. He was born in 1944, taught English literature at Seoul National University, and published three volumes of his own poems. We worked together on a number of translations. This volume was one he particularly cared about.

ing world has grown used to the Japanese word "Zen" to designate Buddhist meditation. For the most part, we have stuck with the corresponding Korean word "Seon," as these are Korean poems.

We noted in the first edition our regret that Allen Ginsberg died before these poems were published. On April 29, 2006, Ko Un was among the poets from around the world who came to New York to pay tribute to Ginsberg on the fiftieth anniversary of the publication of *Howl*.

—BROTHER ANTHONY OF TAIZÉ

Parallax Press, a nonprofit organization, publishes books on engaged Buddhism and the practice of mindfulness by Thich Nhat Hanh and other authors. All of Thich Nhat Hanh's work is available at our online store and in our free catalog. For a copy of the catalog, please contact:

Parallax Press
P.O. Box 7355
Berkeley, CA 94707
Tel: (510) 525-0101
www.parallax.org

Monastics and laypeople practice the art of mindful living in the tradition of Thich Nhat Hanh at retreat communities in France and the United States. To reach any of these communities, or for information about individuals and families joining for a practice period, please contact:

Plum Village
13 Martineau
33580 Dieulivol, France
www.plumvillage.org

Blue Cliff Monastery
3 Mindfulness Road
Pleasant Valley, NY 12566
www.bluecliffmonastery.org

Deer Park Monastery
2499 Melru Lane
Escondido, CA 92026
www.deerparkmonastery.org

For a worldwide directory of Sanghas practicing in the tradition
of Thich Nhat Hanh, please visit www.iamhome.org